Facts About the Sloth Bear

By Lisa Strattin

© 2016 Lisa Strattin

Revised 2022 © Lisa Strattin

FREE BOOK

FREE FOR ALL SUBSCRIBERS

LisaStrattin.com/Subscribe-Here

BOX SET

- FACTS ABOUT THE POISON DART FROGS
- FACTS ABOUT THE THREE TOED SLOTH
- FACTS ABOUT THE RED PANDA
- FACTS ABOUT THE SEAHORSE
- FACTS ABOUT THE PLATYPUS
- FACTS ABOUT THE REINDEER
- FACTS ABOUT THE PANTHER
- FACTS ABOUT THE SIBERIAN HUSKY

LisaStrattin.com/BookBundle

Facts for Kids Picture Books by Lisa Strattin

Little Blue Penguin, Vol 92

Chipmunk, Vol 5

Frilled Lizard, Vol 39

Blue and Gold Macaw, Vol 13

Poison Dart Frogs, Vol 50

Blue Tarantula, Vol 115

African Elephants, Vol 8

Amur Leopard, Vol 89

Sabre Tooth Tiger, Vol 167

Baboon, Vol 174

Sign Up for New Release Emails Here

LisaStrattin.com/subscribe-here

Contents

INTRODUCTION

The Sloth Bear (Melursus ursinus) is a mammal and carnivore belonging to the family Ursidae. This species of bear is the only representative of the genus Melursus. The Sloth Bear is also called Lazy Bear, Honey Bear or long lips Bear.

CHARACTERISTICS

The Sloth Bear is a nocturnal loner that lives in a set territorial area. The territories of males are much larger than that of females. The males and females only find each other during the mating season, and then, the territories of males and females overlap. They don't really hibernate like other bears; however, their activity decreases during the rainy season. Mothers carry their children on their back while foraging for food.

APPEARANCE

The Sloth Bear is blackish colored, rarely dark brown. In the main area of the chest is a white-colored v-shaped or u-shaped band. In rare cases, this band can be missing. The long, pale muzzle is lightly covered with hairs. The coat may be as long as 12 inches around the shoulders. Their nostrils are closed, which is an adaptation to their eating habits. The tongue and the lips are highly extendable. Their teeth are relatively small, considering the size of the animal. The front claws of sloth bears are up to 2-3.4 inches, very long and curved. The soles of the feet are bare of fur and each foot has 5 toes.

LIFE STAGES

The mating season for the Sloth Bear is generally between May and July, and birth of new babies occurs between November to January. Usually, a litter is only 1 to 3 cubs. The birth takes place in a cave, in which the family is living. The male does not participate in the raising of the new babies and has already left the female once they have mated.

The babies weigh just less than one pound and are blind at birth. After about 3 weeks, they open their eyes for the first time. They only leave the cave when they are about two to three months of age and begin to eat solid food. Cubs are weaned at 1.5 or 2.5 years old. They are presumed to be adults at three or four years of age and will have their first birth of their own babies at four or five years old.

LIFE SPAN

This animal has a life expectancy of about 30 years in the wild but may live for more than 30 years in captivity, even up to 40 years.

SIZE

The Sloth Bear reaches a body length of 5 feet or a bit more, a shoulder height of about 2 feet. Head-to tail length is about 4.5 – 6 feet, with a weight of 120 – 300 pounds. Males are as much as 40% heavier than females.

HABITAT

Sloth Bears are native to the Indian subcontinent. Their habitat includes India, Nepal, Bhutan, Bangladesh, and Sri Lanka. In addition to humid rain forests, they also live in and dry, deciduous forests. However, the population density varies in different places depending on food availability.. The animals prefer habitats with dense undergrowth. They don't like open areas at all.

DIET

The food the Sloth Bears like consists mainly of socially organized insects such as ants and termites, as well as sugar-rich fruits. They specifically love to eat honey. With their powerful claws, the animals can easily climb trees to get to the honey bee hives. Ripe fruits are eaten usually from the ground. Termite mounds are broken with their front claws and ant colonies are dug out of the ground. They will eat whatever sugary fruit that is in season where they live.

FRIENDS AND ENEMIES

The Sloth Bear is an endangered species. It has a few natural predators; the tiger and leopard.

The greatest danger to Sloth Bears comes from the destruction of their natural habitats. This is especially true in India and Bangladesh; and beginning to be an issue, as of this writing, in Sri Lanka and Nepal. In designated protected areas, the animals are usually safe.

The total population of the Sloth Bears is estimated at 10,000 to 25,000 animals.

SUITABILITY AS PETS

To many people, owning a pet Sloth Bear seems interesting. However, they can be very noisy and destructive. This means that they could be dangerous around children.

They also get to be pretty big! They are not legal to own in many areas, so you would need to check the local laws where you live before you commit to having this active animal as a pet.

There is also the chance that the pet may get sick and require highly specialized veterinary care, which would not only be expensive but might not even be available in your area. To take care of this, you probably need exotic pet insurance. So, if you want a sloth bear as a pet, you need to make sure you do all the research into these issues.

For most people, the Sloth Bear is not suitable to be a pet. If you want to see them up close, it would be a much better idea to visit a zoo that has an appropriate habitat for them.

COLOR ME

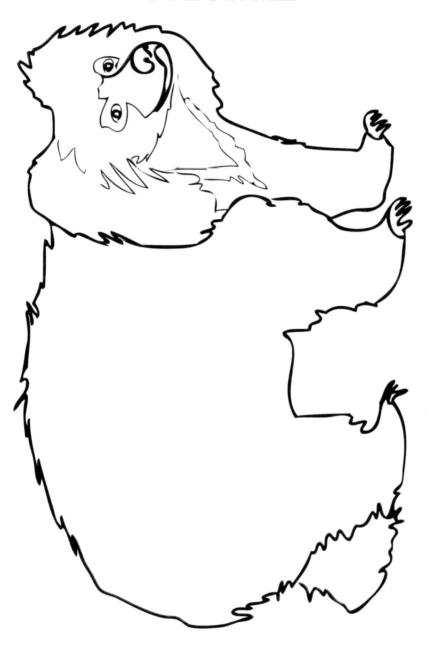

COLOR ME

COLOR ME

COLOR ME

COLOR ME

COLOR ME

COLOR ME

COLOR ME

COLOR ME

COLOR ME

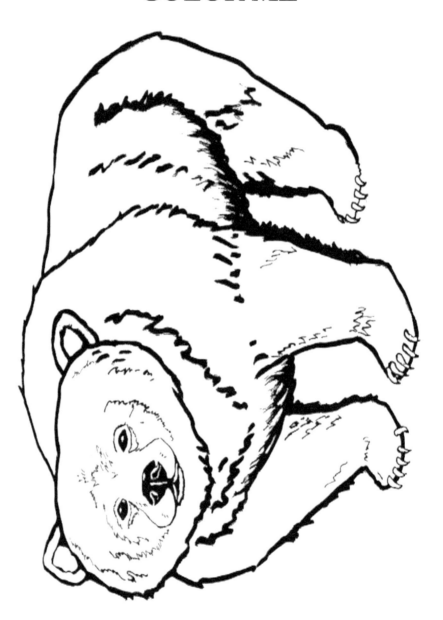

Please leave me a review here:

LisaStrattin.com/Review-Vol-26

For more Kindle Downloads Visit Lisa Strattin Author Page on Amazon Author Central

amazon.com/author/lisastrattin

To see upcoming titles, visit my website at LisaStrattin.com– most books available on Kindle!

LisaStrattin.com

FREE BOOK

FOR ALL SUBSCRIBERS – SIGN UP NOW

LisaStrattin.com/Subscribe-Here

LisaStrattin.com/Facebook

LisaStrattin.com/Youtube

Made in United States
Troutdale, OR
01/08/2025

27762319R00026